Stay in the glory

"And the glory which you gave me I have given them that they may be one just as we are one." (John 17:22)

By

Jennifer Nakuda

All scripture quotations in this book are taken from the King James Version of the Bible unless otherwise indicated

First printing 2021

Second printing 2025

USA Contact:
Tel: +1 945 304 3959
Email: jeniffern2000@gmail.com
Visit My social media:
Instagram: Jennifer Nakuda Author
Facebook: Jennifer Nakuda Author

ISBN: 979-8-89397-434-8

Miracle Center Embassy
Arua, Uganda
Tel: +256 772612656, +256 703656873,
Email: franknankunda@gmail.com

Dedication

I humbly take this grand opportunity to express our gratitude to the man of God who has had the greatest influence upon our lives and ministry through the years, Rev Chris Oyakhilome, DSC, DSc. DD. Thank you dear man of God for always teaching us the timeless truth of God's word in its simplest form, hearing you has brought out the best of God in us. We are forever grateful to God for you Sir. We love you dearly and pray for you always.

Acknowledgments

This book wouldn't be possible without the overwhelming inspiration of the Holy Spirit. What a wonder He has made us! Words will never be able to express it all. I am still a student of the glory He has brought us into. And I am forever grateful to be a child of God.

I'm also very grateful to every one of you ministers of the gospel and children of God that I have had an opportunity to interact with through the years. In one way or another you have played a part in bringing this book to life. A big thank you to Bookwave Publishing for a job well done in refining my words, designing the cover page and publishing a beautiful piece of work. And of course, a mega thank you, to my dear husband, for the unwavering support always.

About the Author

Jennifer Nakuda is an ordained pastor and co-founder, alongside her husband, Frank Nakuda, of Miracle Embassy Church in Uganda, East Africa. Since 2003, she has served in various capacities within the church ministry. Inspired by her interactions with people from all walks of life, Pastor Jennifer has authored six books, offering practical guidance on living a purposeful and fulfilling life. Outside of her ministry work, she is inspired by the beauty of the natural environment, enjoys traveling, and values quality time with family and friends.

Connect with me on Facebook, Instagram or via email:

jeniffern2000@gmail.com

Table of Contents

Introduction

The word glory is usually used in contemporary English to describe an amazing situation of great achievement, however, in the spiritual sense, the word glory goes far beyond to describe a heavenly ambience or presence in a place or upon an individual. This heavenly ambience manifests itself in many ways: perfection, serenity, beauty, splendor, magnificence, wonder, brilliance, excellence, dignity, greatness, honor and much more.

The bible lets us know that the glory of God in the form of a cloud covered the Tabernacle, and the same cloud was over the children of Israel day and night. *"Then the cloud covered the tabernacle and the glorious presence of the Lord filled it. Moses was no longer able to enter the tabernacle because the cloud had settled down over it and the tabernacle was filled with the awesome glory of the Lord. Now whenever the cloud lifted from the tabernacle and moved, the people of Israel would set out on their journey following it. But if the cloud stayed, they would stay until it moved again. The cloud of the lord rested on the tabernacle during the day and at night there was fire in the cloud so all the people of Israel could see it. This continued throughout all their journeys."* (Exodus 40:34-38NLT)

The glory of God as a cloud was God's amazing presence over the Tabernacle and the children of Israel. Everything that is of God carries His glory. The children of Israel being God's own chosen people had the glory surrounding them in the form of a cloud by day and as a pillar of fire by night. His presence around them was a seal of ownership and the guarantee of their safety and well-being. The glory protected and preserved them throughout all their journeys. It is on record that no harm ever befell them. The Bible says they were sustained in the wilderness 40 years lacking nothing, their clothes waxed not old, and their feet swelled not. (Nehemiah 9:21). The glory of God was the air they breathed in and out, and there was not one feeble person among their tribes. (Psalms 105:37)

Over in the New Testament, with the body of Christ specifically, the glory of God is still doing the same and much more.

1

Born into glory

While talking about Jesus, Apostle John lets us know that he was the word of God that became flesh and lived amongst us. And they saw his glory as of the only begotten of the Father full of grace and truth (John 1:14). In other words when they saw Jesus, they saw the glory of God. He was the word made flesh, and the word of God is the glory of God. **"And all of us, as with unveiled face (because we) continue to behold in the word of God) as in a mirror the glory of the Lord…"** 2Cor3:18 AMP

John went ahead to declare, "And of his fullness have all we received, and grace for grace. (John 1:16) Because in Christ, we are born again by the word of God which is the glory of God. *"Being born again not of corruptible seed but of incorruptible by the word of God which lives and abides forever."* (1 Peter 1:23) When we accepted the gospel of Jesus Christ, we were born again by that word of Christ we confessed. Immediately we were translated into the glory of God. *"But we are bound to give thanks always to God for you, brethren beloved of the Lord, because God has from the beginning chosen you to salvation through sanctification of the spirit and belief of the truth; where unto he called you by our gospel to the obtaining of the glory of our Lord Jesus Christ."* (2Thess 2: 13-14)

Therefore, the new creature in Christ, the born-again Christian is the representation of God's glory. As a matter of fact, we are his glory personified. Have you not read that; *"For whom he did foreknow, he also did predestinate to be conformed to the image of his Son that he might be the firstborn among many brethren. Moreover, whom he did predestinate them he also called and whom he called, them he also justified and whom he justified them he also glorified."* (Romans 8:29-30)

The scriptures say the prophets of old searched and inquired to know the times of Christ's suffering leading to his death on the cross and the glory that should come after. *"The Spirit of Christ, which was in them did signify, when it testified before hand the sufferings of Christ and the glory that should follow."* (1Peter 1:10-11) It was prophesied that Jesus Christ would come, die and resurrect from the dead and thereafter it will be a life of glory to whosoever believes in him. Now that he died and risen again, everyone who receives him is born again into glory because he is born of the word and the Spirit of God (1 Cor 12:13).

The glory of God is God's presence that proceeds from His word and His Spirit. The glory of God carries with it the entire heavenly atmosphere filling the person or place with the supernatural aura beyond this world. The Bible says we have this treasure in earthen vessels that the Excellency of the power may be of God and not of us. (2Cor 4:7)

To be born into glory means we are awakened to the fatherhood of God in His kingdom where we fellowship with God Almighty through His word and by His Holy Spirit. Our fellowship with the word and the Holy Spirit of God is the most glorious experience we could ever have. The Spirit of God has always desired to dwell with us, leading and guiding us into paths of righteousness, riches and honor (Proverb 8). This was finally made possible by the death and resurrection of our Lord Jesus Christ.

Now that we are born of the word and the Holy Spirit of God lives in us, the glory and beauty of heaven is in us and with us. We are the image of His glory and beauty in this world. Our continued fellowship with the Word and the Holy Spirit takes us from one level of glory to another. It is called ever-increasing glory! Don't take your fellowship with the Word and the Spirit lightly. He is in us and with us to lead and guide us in this life of glory on the earth. He desires to demonstrate His glory and power through us to this world.

The Holy Spirit of God is so loving, kind and gentle but not amused with sluggishness, complacency and laziness. We must decide deliberately to walk with Him in deep admiration and passion. His desire is to take us from glory to glory in a continuous victory parade. He loves doing exploits and wherever He is highly esteemed, greatness is guaranteed. We must yield ourselves to Him to be able to hear Him in the scriptures, in the preaching of God's word, in prayer, and in the smallest detail of our lives. He is the glory in and of our lives. The most beautiful gift to us from God, the Father. He is the father in us and with us everywhere we are, working in us mightily, demonstrating the glory of God on the earth. This is not for some chosen ones, or a few of His children but all of us, His children, are called and born into His glory.

2

Living in glory

Unlike the children of Israel in the Old Testament, the church of Jesus Christ doesn't have to first see a cloud to know we are in the glory. His glory is in us and with us and we are the manifestation of His glory, everywhere, on this earth. Glory is a realm where we live. This glory emanates from our recreated human spirit that was born anew by the glory of God's word and His spirit. From our recreated human spirit, this glory keeps increasing to affect and impact our sphere of influence. It is our responsibility to keep increasing the glory through fellowship with the Word and the Spirit.

The Bible lets us know that the glory of the New Testament that we have, is far more glorious than the Old Testament glory, which glory, when upon Moses' face the children of Israel could not straightly look at without a veil. *"That old system of law etched in stone led to death, yet it began with such glory that the people of Israel could not bear to look at Moses' face. For his face shone with the glory of God, even though the brightness was already fading away. Shouldn't we expect far greater glory when the Holy Spirit is giving life? If the old covenant, which brings condemnation was glorious, how much more glorious is the new covenant which makes us right with God! In fact, that first glory was not glorious at all compared with the overwhelming glory of the new covenant. So, if the old covenant, which has been set aside, was full of glory, then the new covenant which remains forever has far greater glory. Since this new covenant gives us such confidence, we can be very bold."* (2 Cor 3:7-12 NLT)

Brothers and sisters, we are not ordinary people living in this world. Just like Jesus was when he lived on this earth in the human body, so are we called to live and much more. Everywhere Jesus went the Bible says he was the expression of the Father's glory (Acts 10:38). From healing the sick and feeding thousands, to resurrecting Lazarus buried for four days. Evil forces of darkness bowed at his appearance. The Bible says as he is, so are we in this world (1 John 4:17). We are heirs of God and joint heirs with Christ (Rom 8:17). We are the saviors of this world today. Our purpose is to impose the power and glory of our kingdom on this earth. We are not victims on the earth, and neither are we a batch of people to be pitied. Our lives are hidden with Christ in God (Col 3:3). We are the light of the world (Matthew 5:14), therefore, we are the solution providers of our generation.

When he recognized this greater and overwhelming glory we are called to share in the kingdom, Paul the Apostle of Jesus Christ by the Spirit admonishes us to live our lives worthy of the Lord, reflecting His glory everywhere. *"We pleaded with you, encouraged you, and urged you to live your lives in a way that God would consider worthy; for he called you into his kingdom to share his glory."* (1Thess 2:11-12NLT)

Living in glory and manifesting the glory everywhere, is God's purpose for His children. He wants the whole world to know He is a God of love. The world appreciates what they can see and touch. Multitudes followed Jesus because of what they saw and experienced with him. The glory is tangible as it manifests in miracles, healings, solutions, answers, peace, and much more. The glory solves all man's problems and exalts the God of heaven and earth. Therefore, Apostle Peter reminds us that we have been called to manifest the glory of God in our world.

"But you are a chosen race, a royal priesthood, a dedicated nation, (God's) own purchased, special people; that you may set forth the wonderful deeds and display the virtues and perfections of him who called you out of darkness into his marvelous light," 1Peter 2:9

Though we are in the world, Jesus made it clear that we do not belong to this world, (John 15:19) our purpose here is to display the beauty and perfections, that is to say, the glory of our kingdom so that men will see and fall in love with the God of heaven and earth.

We have been commissioned to teach the world how to live. The world ought to seek solutions for life's problems from us. We are here to teach men how to live gloriously on this earth. Jesus said, *"All power is given unto me in heaven and in earth. Go ye therefore and teach all nations, baptizing them in the name of the Father and of the Son and of the Holy Spirit. Teaching them to observe all things whatsoever I have commanded you and lo, I am with you always even unto the end of the world."* (Matt 28:18-20) Did you see that? No matter where we find ourselves on this earth, we are called to show men how things ought to be done. The excellent and perfect life can only be seen with us children of God. We cannot expect the world to be perfect or show us the most excellent way to do things. We are the wisdom of God personified. Christ was made unto us wisdom (1 Cor 1:30) his wisdom is portrayed through us when we speak and act. The wisdom of this world, the Bible says, comes to nothing. It keeps failing because it is all fleshly, mere human reasoning and understanding. But our wisdom is of God who created the heavens and the earth. He knows all things because He created all things, and today He manifests His wisdom through us to our glory. (1 Cor 2:4-7)

Increasing in glory

Apostle Paul speaking to the church cautions us to hold fast to the teachings of the word; through which we can continuously live and increase in glory. *"But we are bound to give thanks always to God for you, brethren beloved of the Lord, because God has from the beginning chosen you to salvation through sanctification of the spirit and belief of the truth, where unto he called you by our gospel to the obtaining of the glory of our Lord Jesus Christ. Therefore, brethren stand fast and hold the traditions which ye have been taught, whether by word or our epistle."* (2Thess 2: 13-15)

The word of God being the glory of God becomes the manual for our life of glory. In the scriptures, we have all the answers to life's questions and guidelines for this life of glory in Christ. Neglecting the scriptures is neglecting the life of glory. Everything about this life of glory is revealed in the scriptures. The scriptures are not a mere set of rules, they are spirit and life (John 6:63). As we give ourselves to the study of the scriptures, they come alive in our spirit, transforming our mindset to see life from God's perspective which makes it possible for us to live a life guided by the word of God.

The Bible says, *"But we all, with open face beholding as in a glass the glory of the Lord are changed into the same image from glory to glory even as by the Spirit of the Lord."* (2 Cor 3:18) When we look into the scriptures, our spirits get engulfed in the glory we see in the scriptures, causing us to see life through the scriptures. But when we look away from the scriptures, every life situation appears more real resulting into fear, anger, strife etc. Just like the Apostle Peter, while walking on water stopped looking at Jesus the living word, turned his eyes on the storm and immediately started sinking because the storm appeared more real than Jesus' word that called him to walk on water. (Matt 14:30)

But the Bible says, *"While we look not at the things which are seen, but at the things which are not seen; for the things which are seen are temporary, but the things which are not seen are eternal."* (2 Cor 4:18) In the word of God are things that are not seen with physical eyes, yet they are more real and permanent than the situations we face every day. The scripture tells us not to consider those life situations that are seen because they are temporary; they are subject to change at any time by our faith in the word. They are not real, neither are they permanent.

There was a time when the children of Israel were invaded by poisonous snakes that killed all those that were bitten and they cried unto the Lord for help. *"And the Lord said unto Moses, make thee a fiery serpent, and set it upon a pole, and it shall come to pass, that everyone that is bitten, when he looks upon it, shall live. And Moses made a serpent of brass and put it upon a pole and it came to pass, that if a serpent had bitten any man when he beheld the serpent of brass, he lived."* (Numbers 21:8-9) Everyone that looked at the serpent of brass on the pole lived and everyone that chose to look at the snake bite on their body, refusing to look at the brazen serpent on the pole as the word required died.

It doesn't matter what happens around us, we have got to keep our gaze at the glory of the word. *"But we all, with open face beholding as in a glass the glory of the Lord are changed into the same image from glory to glory even as by the Spirit of the Lord."* (2 Cor 3:18) As we behold the glory of the Lord in the word, we are changed into what we see from one level of glory to another by the Spirit of the Lord. It makes no difference what the world says, if it is not in line with the word of God you have no business considering it. Our glory is staying focused onto what the word of God says.

It always touches my heart, every time I read about King Saul, how the Lord had planned to establish his kingdom over Israel forever, but King Saul did not follow God's word to the letter. He chose to listen to the voice of the people instead of following God's word to him. Then came the word of the Lord saying, *"… thou hast done foolishly; thou hast not kept the commandment of the Lord thy God which he commanded thee: for now, would the Lord have established thy kingdom upon Israel forever. But now thy Kingdom shall not continue: the Lord hath sought him a man after his own heart and the Lord has commanded him to be captain over his people because thou hast not kept that which the Lord commanded thee."* (1 Samuel 13:13-14)

God said King Saul did not keep the word given to him, which ended his reign over Israel and the kingdom was given to David. God didn't see it as pressure from the people; He saw King Saul's heart turning to follow the masses because he had no respect for the word of God. Then God said, *"I greatly regret that I have set up Saul as king, for he has turned back from following me, and has not performed my commandments."* (1 Samuel 15: 11) Doing exactly what God had told him to do was the glory of his reign forever. That is what King Saul didn't know that cost him the kingdom.

It is the same thing that happened in the Garden of Eden. The moment Adam listened to the other voice rather than the voice of God that told him not to eat of the fruit, the glory departed. The sad part of all this looking away from the word even for a moment is that most of the consequences are irreversible. It may cause grave penalties for generations to come. For a while everything may remain normal, and no one may even know the danger caused. For example, king Saul remained king over Israel for over 35years though God had rejected him and given the kingdom to another. To God it seemed like there was no king in Isreal until David took over the kingship.

We must stay focused on the word regardless of the cost. As we do, we will only see possibilities, healing, promotion, success and a lot more. It is called dwelling therein meditating on the word day and night. That's our life of glory! It is the same formula of glory and greatness given to all men and women of God that were a wonder to their world in generations gone. He says, *"only be strong and very courageous, that you may observe to do according to all the law, which Moses my servant commanded you; do not turn from it to the right hand or to the left that you may prosper wherever you go."* (Joshua 1:7-9) We have got to be very strong and very courageous to stay on the word regardless of the opposition. It is called "staying in glory."

One inspiring truth about Moses and the word of God is the fact that he saw God's word as his life, not mere words. He once told the children of Israel, *"Set your hearts unto all the words which I testify among you this day, which ye shall command your children to observe to do all the words of this law. For it is not a vain thing for you; because it is your life: and through this thing ye shall prolong your days in the land whither ye go over Jordan to possess it."* (Deuteronomy 32:46-47)

The realm of glory we are born into is more real than the physical world around us. To the one who sees the word as his life and stays therein, the glory of the word becomes more real than the physical world. Everything becomes possible and attainable. In the glory nothing is impossible. The

Bible says *"Blessed is the man who walks not in the counsel of the ungodly, nor stands in the path of sinners, nor sits in the seat of the scornful; But his delight is in the law of the Lord, and in his law, he meditates day and night. He shall be like a tree planted by the rivers of water that brings forth its fruit in its season, whose leaf also shall not wither; and whatever he does shall prosper."* (Psalm 1:1-3)

The greatest temptation for the new creature in Christ is looking away from the glory of the word. Away from the glory is an ordinary life full of struggles, fear, doubt, panic, depression, hatred, unforgiveness, selfishness, lust and every work of darkness. But the one who keeps looking at the glory has no fear of bad news; he's at peace trusting in the Lord of His salvation. *"Thou will keep him in perfect peace whose mind is stayed on thee because he trusts in thee."* (Isa 26:3)

The psalmist painted a beautiful picture of those who dwell in the glory he called it 'the secret place of the most high.' Showing us the kind of life, they enjoy continually saying, *"He who dwells in the secret place of the Most high shall abide under the shadow of the almighty… Because I have made the Lord who is my refuge, even the most high my dwelling place, no evil shall befall me, nor shall any plague come near my dwelling: for he shall give his angels charge over me, to keep me in all my ways. In their hands, they shall bear me up lest I dash my foot against a stone. I shall tread upon the lion and the cobra, the young lion and the serpent I shall trample underfoot. And the Lord says, "Because you have set your love upon me, therefore I will deliver you, I will set you on high, because you have known my name. You shall call upon me and I will answer you; I will be with you in trouble, I will deliver you and honor you. With long life will I satisfy you and show you my salvation."* (Psalms 91NKJV)

Guard your heart with all diligence

"Keep your heart with all diligence for out of it springs the issues of life." (Proverbs 4:20-23 NKJV) It is very important to know that our hearts determine the kind of life we live. Out of the abundance of the heart, the mouth speaks (Luke 6:45). What we meditate on and finally speak is what we create for ourselves whether good or bad. In other words, what we allow into our hearts will define our lives. We are therefore warned to guard our hearts with all diligence. Don't let anything, especially the bad ones settle in there. They will create an unpleasant life for you. A life full of struggles, rejection, anger, pain and penury. Your heart can only produce for you what you sow in there.

God has given us new hearts of flesh that reverence His word just like He promised. *"A new heart also will I give you and a new spirit will I put within you, and I will take away the stony heart out of your flesh, and I will give you an heart of flesh. And I will put my spirit within you and cause you to walk in my statutes and ye shall keep my judgments and do them."* (Ezekiel 36:26-27) Now that this promise is fulfilled in us the born-again Christians, He expects us to guard our hearts protectively by putting off the former manner of life and renewing our minds by the word of God.

Every time we open our hearts to rumors and deception, betrayal, pain and sorrow, fear and worry, anger and bitterness, strife and pride, we make it difficult for the word to produce in us what it talks about. We instead open a door for the adversary to torment and hinder the flow of God's blessings into our lives. Always remember Satan came to steal, kill and destroy (John 10:10). If the devil can succeed in stealing the word from you, and ensure it never reaches your heart, then he has got you right where he wants you, in order to cause death and destruction of anything that matters to you.

Jesus once told a parable of a Sower who went to sow seed, and he said the seed was the word of God. He said some seeds fell on good ground, others fell on the wayside, others on the stony places and others among thorns. It really matters where the seed of God's word falls. As children of the word, we must always keep our hearts as good ground for the word to sprout and produce for us hundred-fold harvest (Matt 13).

The word of God is not difficult for us children of God to understand, and neither are we strangers to the word. The word of God gave birth to us in Christ. *"Of his own will begat he us with the word of truth, that we should be a kind of first fruit of his creatures."* (James 1:18) We are the offspring of the word; we are one with the word. We can understand it much more than any world scholar of divinity. The anointing of His Spirit in us teaches us all things. *"But the anointing which ye have received of him abides in you and ye need not that any man teaches you but as the same anointing teaches you of all things and is truth and is no lie and even as it has taught you ye shall abide in him."* (1 John 2:27) You need not any man outside of Christ to teach you because he has not the anointing of his Spirit. Over here in Christ, He has given us gifts of men to perfect the saints. *"And he gave some apostles; and some prophets; and some evangelists; and some pastors and some teachers; For the perfecting of the saints, for the work of the ministry, for the edifying of the body of Christ."* (Eph 4:11-12)

The enemy plans to make sure you never find out the truth about this life of glory. He will make you think the Bible is a very lengthy book that is hard to read and finish, or it is too complicated to be understood. He will tell you that the Bible is very confusing and full of contradictions, you will never be able to grasp a thing in it. With such deception, many have turned away from the Bible before they ever started to read.

This is all a big lie from the father of lies who wants you out of the glory life. He enjoys keeping humanity in the darkness where he can inflict pain and sorrow. He will ensure people never find out or at least they will reject the revealed truth and follow a lie. That's how he has been able to destroy many lives from generation to generation by blinding men's hearts from the truth (2 Cor 4:4) or by twisting the truth so that men never get to order their lives by the truth of God's word. For example, in Genesis 3:4 the devil told Eva that they would not surely die. But they died, both spiritually and physically on the same day (2Peter3:8). And death continued to all generations.

But Jesus said, ye shall know the truth and the truth shall make you free. (John 8:32) To know the truth is every Christian's privilege and responsibility too. The truth is revealed to us in the scriptures and everyone who desires to know the truth goes to the scriptures to discover for themselves and they never walk in darkness again.

Jesus said whosoever follows him shall never walk in darkness but shall have the light of life (John 8:12). This literary means whosoever follows him, shall never walk in ignorance but shall be illuminated, knowing the truth about life. We follow him in his word because he is his word. In us is the ability to follow his voice just like the sheep follow the shepherd. (John 10:1-5).

We train our hearts to walk in the light of God's word no matter what happens or whatever others say. For example, Jesus knew Judas would betray him nevertheless he shared with him on the same plate and kissed him to show us that the enemy will always be close, but he is not a factor; only remain focused on walking in the light of God's word.

No amount of evil can resist the power of God's word. No need to get into rage, hatred, bitterness, vowing never to be nice to people again because they took advantage of your kindness. This will only bind you and hinder your progress. It is so sad that this is where the devil has locked many of God's children frustrating their lives and destroying their future.

This reminds me of how a prophet went to Jesse's house to anoint a future king. Upon looking at the first-born Eliab, the prophet declared him the lord's anointed just by looking at his face and stature. However, God immediately interrupted the prophet saying don't anoint him for I have rejected him. And went on to say, ***"The Lord does not look at the things man looks at. Man looks at the outward appearance, but the lord looks at the heart."*** (1 Sam 16:7 NIV). This reveals how important the state of our heart is to God. May God always find in you and me a heart after His own heart! Not one full of anger, bitterness, jealousy and unforgiveness. Eliab lost the right to kingship as firstborn because of what was in his heart. God couldn't work with him and couldn't trust him with His people as king because of his heart.

The sooner we discover that the only enemy we have is the old serpent, the devil, whose mission is to steal, kill and destroy, the quicker we learn to take no offence. Demons are spirits; they may go through anyone to get to you. It is your responsibility to stop them from affecting your heart. That same devil once used Peter to get to Jesus with worldly counsel, but Jesus was smarter and rebuked Satan (Matt 16:21-23). Our anger should be directed at the devil and his demons, commanding them to get out of our way. Knowing the real enemy empowers us to enjoy our life of glory, free from any form of bondage, walking in love always.

Rooted in him

As ye have therefore received Christ Jesus the Lord, so walk ye in him: rooted and built up in him, and stablished in the faith, as ye have been taught, abounding therein with thanksgiving. Beware lest any man spoil you through philosophy and vain deceit, after the tradition of men, after the rudiments of the world and not after Christ. (Col 2: 6-8)

It is important that after coming to Christ, you walk in him, rooted and built up in the faith. Otherwise, you will be drawn away by the deception in the world and the traditions of men that appeal to the senses but never provide lasting solutions to life situations.

When Jesus was confronted by the religious leaders of his day for not following the traditions of men, he rebuked them for laying aside God's word to esteem and teach the traditions of men. He quoted the prophet Isaiah who called them hypocrites that honour God with their lips, but their hearts are far from him. He said they worship God in vain and make the word of God of no effect because of their traditions. (Mark 7:5-13)

If after coming to Christ we insist on keeping and following the cultures and traditions of men, we are no different from the Pharisees that Jesus rebuked. We will be like them, hypocrites, that talk about God's word but living a different kind of life. And more importantly those cultures and traditions hinder the power of God's word from working in our lives. The word of God cannot manifest its power in the life of a man or woman that considers the traditions of men to be important. God desires that after we have come to Him, the word of God becomes our way of life. The only way we should live.

Walk in the newness of life

"What shall we say then? Shall we continue in sin, that grace may abound? God forbid. How shall we that are dead to sin, live any longer therein? Know ye not, that so many of us as were baptized into Jesus Christ were Baptized into his death? Therefore, we are buried with him by baptism into death: that like as Christ was raised up from the dead by the glory of the father, even so we also should walk in newness of life." (Romans 6:1-4)

In Christ, we have a new life of glory that has power over sin. When the first man Adam sinned, man fell from glory but when Jesus died and rose again, he brought everyone who believed in him back into glory. (Romans 3:23-24) We are expected to walk in the newness of life filled with glory because that is what Grace has done for us. Grace has given us the ability to say no to sin and live a righteous and glorious life in Christ.

It is only those who are ignorant of God's word that still have issues with sin. But those who have yielded themselves to the glory of God's word have subdued the power of sin, dominating its influence thereof. David revealed a secret of all time that overpowers sin when he declared to God, "Thy word have I hid in mine heart that I might not sin against you." (Psalms 119:11) Those that hide the word of God in their hearts, walk in dominion over sin and its consciousness. The problem of many is not even sin itself but the consciousness of sin. They go about worrying if they have sinned yet or not. They refer to themselves as sinners who need grace to survive, not knowing they are talking themselves out of grace for dominating sin. In Christ we have received grace to rule over sin (Romans 5:14)

What the Christian ought to say is, 'I am the righteousness of God saved by grace I have dominion over sin. The more we say it, the more we create the picture of who we are in our mind. This is what defeats and paralyzes sin and the works of evil. Fear and consciousness of sin have taken many back into bondage from whence they were set free by Christ. They still think they are mere human beings subject to sin. That is why the spirit tells us to renew our minds with the Word so that we will know the good and perfect will of God. *"And be not conformed to this world but be ye transformed by the renewing of your mind, that ye may prove what is that good, and acceptable, and perfect will of God."* (Rom 12:2)

He doesn't want us to conform to this world, thinking and talking like them. We are no longer of this world. In Christ, we have become completely new people without a past, the sinful nature of the past life was taken away (Col 2:11-12 NLT). We ought to know we have come into the kingdom of God and received a new nature of righteousness. We live our lives according to our new nature of righteousness in Christ (Eph 4:24). The nature of sin has been removed therefore sin has no power over us. (Rom 6:14)

Just because we have a human body, it doesn't make us subject to sin. Jesus was God living in a human body but in him was nothing found of the devil (John 14:30). Sin is of the devil; we have no business entertaining even a slight thought from the kingdom of Satan. It should be strange for a Christian to sit down and start planning how to tell a lie as though it is normal.

This ignorance of our dominion over sin has made many children of God to strongly identify themselves with their earthly lineage, tribes and nations calling themselves 'son of the soil,' or 'born of so and so tribe or nation.' As innocent and patriotic as this may sound, it is the reason for the stagnation, ineffectiveness and spiritual weakness among the children of God.

Many still carry native names that are rooted in witchcraft, idol worship and bad lack. Every time they answer the name; it is a bad environment they create around themselves. Words have meanings that become a reality every time they are spoken out. Every child of God should be careful of the associations they choose to belong. Associations have spirits that follow and manifest in the lives of the members. Identifying yourself with the old life where Christ got you from is falling from grace. It is making Christ and his word of no effect in your life. You cannot agree to both the old lifestyle and the new one and be a success with God.

Jesus said you can't serve two masters at ago. You will either love the one or hate the other, or you will hold on to the one and despise the other (Matt 6:24). That's the very reason you will find those that you thought were good Christians paying strong allegiance to the systems and dictates of the wisdom of this world more than what God says.

They started out by missing church service occasionally until it became normal not to go to church when they don't feel like it. It is not difficult for them to choose the wisdom of men over God's wisdom. To them, the things of the spirit are not a priority, and they are not bothered by their fleshly way of living. They are not ashamed to cancel a church meeting to attend to their personal issues, or something worldly, just to appease their non-Christian friends or family.

One can simply say these kinds of people added God to their lives instead of giving their lives to God, there is a very big difference. If we say we gave God our lives, we ought to show it. Because it means He owns us. He is the boss. We do what He wants. He must be first in our lives and His ways become our ways.

But if we have the audacity to choose our own way over His, it simply means we just added Him to our lives like one would find another friend to join his circle of friends. This doesn't work with God. He is either the Lord of our lives or not the Lord at all. He wants to be the only master we serve. He has brought us into a life of glory. He wants us to remain therein and enjoy the liberty and the overflowing of grace. Serving other masters and choosing our own way over His only messes up our life of glory. We were born again for his glory and that's who He wants us to be always; a holy nation, a peculiar people, beautified and gloried for Him alone.

Be fully persuaded

We have to be totally convinced that God is who He says He is, and we are what He says we are. Although we are all born again into glory, this life of glory is only witnessed by sons and daughters with conviction. There are many distractions and challenges that are intended to draw our attention from the glory but if you have got your spirit and soul convinced that God's word is all powerful and its final, you will stick with it and enjoy this life of glory.

The children of Israel could not enter the Promised Land flowing with milk and honey because they could not be persuaded. It was so difficult to get the children of Israel to believe that God had given them the Promised Land because of the presence of giants. Today we are born into this Promised Land of glory but how persuaded are we of this truth? How much have we believed in this glorious life? Is it more real to you than the challenges of life? The Bible says because they could not be persuaded God was angry with that entire generation and they all perished in the wilderness apart from their children who knew nothing, and Joshua and Caleb who dared to believe God.

The wilderness was never meant to be a place of abode for the children of Israel. It was only a route they had to take to avoid interference from other nations on their way to the promised land. But they stayed there for 40 years because of their unbelief. They didn't move until the last person of the unbelieving generation died.

In the same way, the children of Israel didn't have to stay in the wilderness for 40 years, we too in Christ have no business with any wilderness, whatsoever. First, we are not going to any promised land, we are born again into that land (Heb 12: 22-24). Secondary, in that land there is no wilderness. Most of the "unpleasant" situations that we experience as children of God are training or nurturing experiences in which we are expected to do the word of God and move on to higher realms of glory. If you check with the scriptures, you will discover there's a word for every situation in life.

Whatever word it is for your situation, if you receive it in your spirit, it will bring peace beyond human understanding and joy unspeakable and full of glory. The situation may not change immediately or at all. But here you are at peace and joyful because you know that in all these things you are more than a conqueror for greater is He that is in you than He that is in the world (1John 4:4). If you stay in the word, you will surely live in glory all your life.

Jesus also had a share of his 'unpleasant experience', after he was baptized of John, the Bible says, *"immediately the Spirit drove him into the wilderness. And he was there in the wilderness forty days, tempted of Satan; and was with the wild beasts; and the angels ministered unto him."* (Mark 1:12-13) I believe, one of the major reasons Jesus was in the wilderness praying and fasting was spiritual training, learning to win with the word of God under any circumstance. It is at this point that we see him face to face with Satan and the wild beasts and after taming them with the word, the angels ministered to him. *"Again, the devil took him up on an exceedingly high mountain and showed him all the kingdoms of the world and their glory. And he said to him, "all these things I will give you if you bow down and worship me" Then Jesus said to him, away with you Satan! For it is written, you shall worship the Lord your God and him only you shall serve. Then the devil left him and behold angels came and ministered to him."* (Matt 4:8-11)

The Bible lets us know that though Jesus was a Son, yet he learnt obedience in the things that he suffered. (Heb 5:8) He learnt to dominate unpleasant situations like hunger for 40 days standing on the word. (Matt 4:2-4) He refused to bow down and worship Satan for the kingdoms of the world and their glory, insisting on worshipping God alone. (Matt 4:8-10) Just like Jesus, we are expected to stand on the word of God amidst strong opposition.

In Christ, we are born right into glory; we carry our own atmosphere of glory infused with power and authority. Our life journey is from one level of glory to another as we go through different stages of spiritual growth. The quicker, we are persuaded that the word of God is final and choose to live by it, refusing to bow to the circumstances of life, the faster we move to the next level of glory in Christ; and the glory just keeps increasing as we stay in the word of God.

Choose the way of the word and you will keep moving to greater glory in Christ. God expects all His children to operate at higher realms of glory. The calm and cool Christianity without the display of power and glory is not God's will for His children. For that matter, the Bible warns us not to fall into the same temptation of unbelief that the children of Israel suffered for 40 years until they died without ever enjoying the land flowing with milk and honey.

"(Therefore beware) brethren, take care lest there be in any one of you a wicked, unbelieving heart (which refuses to cleave to, trust in and rely on him) leading you to turn away and desert or stand aloof from the living God. but instead warn one another every day as long as it is called today that none of you may be hardened (into settled rebellion) by the deceitfulness of sin. For we have become fellows with Christ and share in all he has for us, if only we hold our first newborn confidence and original assured expectation, firm and unshaken to the end." (Hebrews 3:12-14 AMP)

God has given us everything we will ever require living this life of glory without excuse. The Bible says, ***"his divine power hath given unto us all things that pertain unto life and godliness, through the knowledge of him that hath called us to glory and virtue"*** (2 Peter 1:3). Did you see that? We must know the one who has called us to a life of glory and excellence. We know Him through the word. Knowing Him unveils to us this life of glory filled with all the things we will ever need in life and for godliness. As we continue to walk in the light of His word, our path is likened unto the shining light that shines more and more unto the perfect day. (Proverbs 4:18)

3

Discerning the body of Christ

When talking about living in glory, discerning or understanding the body of Christ is very important. Many have not understood the body of Christ and have brought judgment on themselves. The body of Christ is the most glorious entity on this earth. The Bible says we are *"a chosen generation, a royal priesthood a holy nation, a peculiar people..."* (1 Peter 2:9). We are not ordinary people on the earth. We are born of God. We have the life (1 John 5:11) and nature of God (2 Peter 1:4). We are gods (Psalms 82:6).

Our oneness with the Lord cannot be ignored or underestimated. It is what makes us extraordinary in this world. We are one spirit with the Lord (1 Cor 6:17). Jesus made it clear that He is the vine, and we are the branches. The vine and its branches are the same. They share the same life. This is one of the strongest reasons we take the Holy Communion; to declare and affirm our oneness with Him. He said, *"Whoever eats my flesh and drinks my blood remains in me and I in him."* (John 6:56)

That is why Apostle Paul warns the church not to take the Holy Communion unworthily, dishonoring the body of Christ. He says, *"Therefore whosoever eats this bread or drinks this cup of the Lord in an unworthy manner will be guilty of the body and blood of the Lord. But let a man examine himself and so let him eat of the bread and drink of the cup. For he who eats and drinks in an unworthy manner eats and drinks judgment to himself not discerning the Lord's body. For this reason, many are weak and sick among you, and many sleep. For if we would judge ourselves, we would not be judged. But when we are judged we are chastened by the Lord, that we may not be condemned with the world. Therefore, my brethren, when you come together to eat, wait for one another. But if anyone is hungry, let him eat at home, lest you come together for judgment."* (1 Cor 11:26-34)

When the Lord said we should have Holy Communion, to proclaim his death till he comes; it was also going to be a constant reminder of our oneness with Him. Holy Communion is a symbol of our sharing together in his death, burial and resurrection. He was on the cross as our representative. He was dying in our place; we died on the cross in him and rose again in him. Every time we take the Holy Communion; we announce his death in our place which set us free from sin and death making us one righteous body in him at his resurrection.

Apostle Paul was therefore concerned that the brethren were taking Holy Communion unworthily as if it was an ordinary meal. The Apostle advised the brethren to first eat in their homes to ease the hunger before coming for Holy Communion; so that they don't take condemnation instead of a blessing.

Holy Communion is to be taken in reverence remembering what Jesus did for us, declaring and affirming the New Testament blessings in our lives as members of the body of Christ. But the brethren had turned it into an ordinary feast of first come first serve. They ate to fill their stomachs without considering if others had their share or not. And this is what Paul called 'eating the bread and drinking the cup' unworthily, leading to condemnation.

The Bible says, *"The cup of blessing which we bless, is it not the communion of the blood of Christ? The bread which we break, is it not the communion of the body of Christ? For we being many are one bread, and one body; for we are all partakers of that one bread."* (1 Cor 10:16-17) We are all partakers of that one bread from heaven Jesus Christ. *"We are members of his body of his flesh and of his bones."* (Eph 5:30)

A very important lesson for us to learn here is that every time we don't understand the sacredness of the body of Christ, and we dishonor each other like the Corinthian brethren did while taking Holy Communion, we bring judgment on ourselves as members of the body of Christ. For that very reason, the Bible says many are weak, sickly and even die. In other words, many are weak in their faith, become sickly and even die for not treating each other with honor.

The Spirit therefore says if we would examine ourselves and judge the way we relate and treat the members of the body of Christ, we will not be judged by the Lord. *"For if we would judge ourselves, we would not be judged..."* (1Cor 11:31) For that same reason we are advised to have godly reverence for one another as the body of Christ that we will not fall into judgment

The body of Christ that we are is a sacred entity to be handled with honor and much reverence. *"For as the body is one and has many members and all the members of that one body, being many, are one body so also is Christ. for by one Spirit are we all baptized into one body, whether we be Jews or Gentiles, whether we be bond or free; and have been all made to drink into one Spirit. For the body is not one member but many. If the foot shall say because I am not the hand I am not of the body, is it therefore not of the body? And if the ear shall say because I am not the eye, I am not of the body is it therefore not of the body? If the whole body were an eye, where was the hearing? If the whole body were hearing, where was the smelling? But now has God set the members every one of them in the body as it has pleased him. And if they were all one member, where were the body? But now are they many members yet but one body. And the eye cannot say unto the hand I have no need of thee; nor again the head to the feet, I have no need of you. Nay much more those members of the body which seem to be more feeble are necessary. And those members of the body which we think to be less honorable, upon these we bestow more abundant honor and our uncomely parts have more abundant comeliness. For our comely parts have no need; but God has tempered the body together, having given more abundant honor to that part which lacked. That there should be no division in the body; but that the members should have the same care one for another. And whether one member suffer, all the members suffer with it; or one member be honored all the members rejoice with it. Now ye are the body of Christ and members in particular."* (1 Cor 12: 12-27)

We are the body of Christ and members in particular Hallelujah! Just because we are different parts of the body performing unique functions, it doesn't mean we are separate from the body. We are the body of Christ and He is the head (Eph 1:22-23). While praying for us Jesus said, *"I have given them the glory that you gave me, that they may be one as we are one. I in them and you in me, May they be brought to complete unity to let the world know that you sent me and have loved them even as you have loved me."* (John 17:22-23 NIV)

Our understanding of the master's desire for us to be in unity and harmony with each other keeps us in glory. We are children of one Father who has sent us on a mission in the world to represent him. He has given everyone a part to play in this mission and expects each one of us to focus on that assignment just like every part of the body keeps to its assignment for the good of the body. The hand doesn't question the leg because they all get instruction from the central nervous system and report back to the same system.

Jesus is the head of the body and in charge of the central nervous system. The hand may never understand how the stomach digests the food, but the head (master) operates it all. The body remains strong and healthy when every part is playing its role. And if any part of the body stops playing its role, the whole body has to face the consequences. Though we have different assignments we are all coordinated and kept healthy and strong when we all focus on our purpose in life. This is one way to bless each other by staying in our purpose and fulfilling it without murmuring, grumbling and complaining about other members' assignments. That's when the world will look at us and know we are indeed of the same father just like Jesus prayed for us.

If you don't agree with what your brother is doing and you are really concerned, reach him and find out what he has to say about your concerns instead of fighting him without knowledge of your brother's intentions. If after talking with him you still don't reach an agreement, pray for him and then leave the matter to God and continue to focus on your own assignment.

Always avoid giving a personal opinion on your brother's work because to his master our master he reports. We may not agree but it doesn't call for a fight or public opposition. Our kingdom is not a democracy that we all first vote who God is going to use next and how. The father decides who to use and how. He wants us all to focus on our different assignments.

This brings to mind one of the Master's interesting conversations with Apostle Peter after the resurrection. In this particular conversation Jesus was specifically assigning the Apostle to his life purpose explaining to him how it would be to the end. The Apostle just like many of us wanted to know what would happen to another disciple who was close by and asked Jesus what would become of that particular disciple. The master straight away told him it's none of your business. *"Then Peter turning about sees the disciple whom Jesus loved following…. Peter seeing him said to Jesus, Lord and what shall this man do? Jesus said unto him, if I will that he tarry till I come, what is that to thee? Follow thou me."* (John 21:20-22) The master clearly indicated that what He chooses to do with another is all up to Him. What He wants from each of us is to follow Him without looking around into other people's assignments. We are all one big family of God. He gives His children assignments according to His design. He only desires unity amongst us.

We should be ashamed to raise a figure or open our mouths to speak about our fellow brothers and sisters in the Lord regardless of the situation. The Love which is given to us by the Holy Ghost covers a multitude of sins. David protected Saul as much as Saul wanted to kill him. David had respect for the anointing that was poured upon King Saul.

Even though God later rejected Saul and anointed David in his place, David refused to raise his figure or mouth against the Lord's anointed. David didn't dare judge King Saul for his shortcomings in the kingship; he left that to Saul and God. David maintained one fact 'Saul had been anointed of God' to the extent that David and his men fasted and mourned the death of Saul; and had the man killed who braggingly reported Saul's death to David. (1Sam 24:4-7, 2 Sam 1:1-16)

King David was a man of God who had high regard for spiritual things. He understood the blessing of honoring God's people. He knew that God permitted no man to harm His people and even rebuked kings for their sakes, *"saying, do not touch my anointed ones, and do my prophets no harm."* (1 Chronicles 16:22) That warning was specific to the heathen not to touch the children of Israel because they were a chosen people, anointed of God and prophets of God. David understood that even the anointed was not permitted to touch another anointed and he left Saul alone.

In the same way that God allowed no man to touch the Israelites because they were chosen, anointed and prophetic, it is the same way God has not permitted anyone to touch the body of Christ because we are chosen, anointed and prophetic. Many don't understand that the body of Christ is a body of anointed prophets. The entire body is anointed by virtue of the Holy Spirit that dwells in us and we are all prophets by the same Holy Spirit that lives in us.

He said, *"And it shall come to pass afterward that I will pour out my spirit upon all flesh; and your sons and your daughters shall prophesy, your old men shall dream dreams, your young men shall see visions."* (Joel 2:28) Whether they are the prophets in the office of the prophet or the rest of us prophets that speak words of power by the Holy Spirit, he says touch not my anointed ones and do my prophets no harm for your own good. That is why many are weak, and sickly and some die for not understanding the glory of the body of Christ.

Fighting and attacking one another whether privately or publicly is not allowed in the body of Christ. Refuse to be a pollutant of the body of Christ; choose to love and not to hate no matter what is done to you. Choose to remain in the glory. Don't let other Christians' mistakes and faults become your topic of discussion.

Don't allow the spirit of pride to turn you into a critic always judging what others are doing. The best you can do to help is pray for the body of Christ. *"There is one lawgiver, who is able to save and to destroy; who are you to judge another."* (James 4:12) God doesn't have to first consult with anyone before He works with another. Our responsibility is to focus on our assignments and love one another as a body of anointed saints and prophets of God. Our extraordinary power to change this world is in our unity as the body of Christ.

Jesus foretold what would happen at the final judgment saying, *"And the king will answer and say to them, assuredly, I say to you, in as much as you did it to one of the least of these my brethren, you did it to me."* (Matt 25:40) Good or bad, whatever is done to his brethren is done unto him. When Jesus met Saul on his way to Damascus to persecute the Christians, he didn't ask him why he persecuted the Christians. He said, *"Saul Saul, why are you persecuting me? And he said; who are you, Lord? Then the Lord said, 'I am Jesus whom you are persecuting."* (Acts 9:4-5NIV) That is the reality of our oneness with him. Whosoever touches us, touches him.

We should esteem all the children of God and highly esteem those that are over us in the Lord, honoring one another for we all carry God in us. *"And we beseech you brethren to know them which labour among you and are over you in the Lord and admonish you; and <u>to esteem them very highly in love for their work's sake and be at peace among yourselves.</u> Now we exhort you brethren, warn them that are unruly, comfort the feebleminded, support the weak, and be patient toward all men. See that none render evil for evil unto any man; but ever follow that which is good, both among yourselves and to all men."* (1Thessalonians 5: 12-15)

4

Reverently handle the sacred things

As a body of Christ, everything about us is sacred. Knowing this truth helps us to relate reverently with the sacred things in and around us for our good. Our consciousness of this reality enhances an atmosphere of ever-increasing glory full of the miraculous.

First and foremost, the number one most sacred thing is YOU the child of God, in whom the Holy Spirit of God dwells. We are consecrated unto God. It really matters how we conduct ourselves privately or publicly. We are the only holy people on the face of the earth. *"Ye are a chosen generation, a royal priesthood <u>an holy nation,</u>"* (1 Peter 2:9).

Apostle Paul makes it even clearer when he helps us understand that we are not our own saying, *"Know ye not that your body is the temple of the Holy Ghost which is in you, which ye have of God, and ye are not your own? For ye are bought with a price therefore glorify God in your body and in your spirit which are God's."* (1 Cor 6:19-20) As the temple of the Holy Spirit, everything about us is in service to God, to glorify God and to increase glory in us.

It is therefore important as consecrated people to know that we do not own ourselves anymore. We were bought with a price; we belong to God. Our lives are hidden with Christ in God (Col 3:3). We should thus behave and conduct ourselves in a manner that glorifies God in our lives. The Bible says, *"Whatsoever ye do in word or deed, do all in the name of the Lord Jesus, giving thanks to God and the Father by him."* (Col 3:17)

"Do all things without murmurings and disputing; that ye may be blameless and harmless, the sons of God without rebuke in the midst of a crooked and

perverse generation among whom ye shine as lights in this world, holding the word of life... " (Philippians 2:14-16)

"For the lips of a priest should keep knowledge, and from his mouth men should seek instruction because he is the massager of the Lord almighty." (Mal 2:7) For this very reason we have been made priests unto God; to keep knowledge and to instruct people about life. We don't speak what they want to hear but what God wants them to hear. We speak God's mind in every situation as His children. And we are admonished to keep away from those whose communication is contrary to the wisdom of God. *"Be not deceived; evil communications corrupt good manners. Awake to righteousness and sin not for some have not the knowledge of God..."* (1 Cor 15:33-34)

Secondly, because we are holy and carry the presence of God, everything connected to us is by virtue consecrated. They all receive a rub-off of the glory of God that we carry. Take for example the homes we reside in, they become holy habitations because of our presence. Therefore, the people and things we allow into our homes whether physically or via other sources like media must be those that enhance the glory in our lives and homes or at least those that are under our influence.

As holy people, we have numerous holy angels that go with us and keep us by our homes. They ought to minister for us in an enabling environment (Heb 1:14). The more conscious we are of these facts, the more glory we enjoy and demonstrate in our lives. That's the reason for our neatness, excellence, cleanliness, decency, smartness etc. The Bible says we should carry out our salvation with godly reverence. (Philippians 2:12NLT)

Thirdly, our children too are holy (I Corinthians 7:14) and this calls for godly consciousness as we raise them in the fear of the Lord. They are royalty and should be brought up that way with dignity and excellence. Not fearful and timid but knowing who they are in Christ; children that honor and have high regard for spiritual things.

It is every guardian and parent's responsibility to raise their children in the way of the Lord that they ought to go and when they are old, they will never depart from it. (Prov 22:6) Children are God's heritage to us, intended to bring us lasting joy, they are for signs and wonders. It is not fair enough to entirely blame the children for not turning out the way we expected them. Parents have a big role in the children's upbringing that goes beyond providing food, shelter and clothing. Parents are their first spiritual role models. They don't only watch and learn most of the things from their parents, but most importantly children hold their parents in high regard as superheroes in everything.

Fourthly, our places of worship are holy just like our meetings are holy gatherings of saints in which the Lord Almighty dwells, *"For where two or three are gathered together in my name, there am I in the midst of them"* (Matt 18:20). Imagine if we all had this consciousness that God is in our midst every time we gather, many would never miss church service because they are not feeling well. They would be the first in church knowing they won't go back the same.

Anyone walking into the gathering of the brethren burdened by the cares of this world, ought to be lifted immediately by the glory in our midst. Sickness ought to go by coming into the holy gathering of the saints. But when we are not conscious of the glory we carry, some come in and behave like they just joined a village chief's meeting. It should not be so, we ought to be conscious of the glory we carry and His presence in our midst. This makes every meeting a life-changing experience for everybody.

Number five is the altar. The altar is holy, and the offerings are holy. This calls for reverence while handling the altar and the offerings thereof. How we handle and treat the offerings is very important. When the offering is still in your hands you have the choice to do whatever you want with it, but once it touches the altar, just let it be. Your next responsibility is to receive the blessings that follow. Leave the rest to the minister appointed to handle the offerings. To whom it is required to reverently handle as instructed by the senior minister according to God's word.

This is very important to understand because many lives have been gravely affected by mishandling the offerings. All types of offerings including the tithe, and first fruits are an act of worship unto God by the giver. Make no mistakes about this; giving of offerings is very sacred for us as priests unto God. Everyone handling offerings ought to know that offerings are holy sacrifices unto God. To take another person's worship and sacrifice to God lightly is not a good idea.

The tithe belongs to God. We pay it for our own good. Out of all that God gives us, He expected 10% to connect our resources to a lasting blessing without a devourer in the monetary system of this world. He says, *"bring ye all the tithe into the storehouse that there may be meat in my house and prove me now herewith says the Lord of host, if I will not open you the window of heaven and pour you out a blessing that there shall not be room enough to receive it. And I will rebuke the devourer for your sake…and all nations shall call you blessed; for you shall be a delightsome land says the Lord of host."* (Mal 3:10-12)

The first fruits are offerings of honor that bring an increase in our lives and open up new horizons of operations. To ignore the first fruit is to ignore the increase and new opportunities. *"Honor the Lord with thy substance and with all the first fruit of thy increase. So, shall thy barns be filled with plenty and thy presses shall burst out with new wine."* (Proverbs 3:9-10)

5

Conclusion

God has called us to a life of glory, and it is our responsibility to stay in the glory and enjoy the blessings thereof. This book was written to draw our attention to what we have and how to keep it. The Lord rebukes those he loves *"for the Lord corrects and disciplines everyone whom he loves and he punishes every son he accepts"* (Heb 12:6 AMP). Reading this book is proof of God's love and His desire to keep us in the right way.

Jesus told a parable of the prodigal son simply to show how much the Father is always willing to restore us. The Bible says the prodigal son came back to his senses and said, in my father's house there's plenty for everyone including the servants and here I am eating pigs' food. I will go back to my father. (Luke 15:11-32)

The life of glory we are born into means only glory and nothing less; the glory only keeps increasing from time to time as we grow in the knowledge of our Lord Jesus Christ. Outside the glory is the adversary roaring like a lion looking for whom to devour. One act of compromise can open up for the adversary. Once the door is opened and the adversary is not cast out immediately, suffering may go from bad to worse as many more evil spirits join the first one to cause havoc.

In ignorance, the Christian will be confused and wondering why the suffering and seemingly bad luck everywhere forgetting a door was opened. The Bible says, "Give no place to the devil" (Eph 4:27) because he will want to take over everything.

It doesn't matter how much damage is done already and how long it has been, when you come back to your senses and realize this is the devil at work, do what James 4:7 says, submit yourselves to God (to His word), resist the devil and He will flee from you. Do all you have got to do to cast him out. For some that's all it takes to get back to glory. For others, it might require putting things right with some people or discontinuing from certain ways in order to close the door and start enjoying the glorious life. God is not willing that His children should suffer in any way or even perish. The only suffering permitted is persecution for living godly in Christ. (2 Tim 3:12).

Jesus came that we might have life to the full. But the devil comes to steal kill and destroy (John 10:10). The devil's major agenda is to destroy. Don't let him accomplish his mission in you. Cast him out. The devil may have afflicted your body, finances, marriage, mention it, it doesn't matter; in you is the power to bring the restoration. Tell the devil to leave your body, finances, home, business, ministry and he will go in Jesus name. *"And these signs shall follow them that believe: in my name shall they cast out devils: they shall speak with new tongues: they shall take up serpents and if they drink any deadly thing it shall not hurt them. They shall lay hands on the sick and they shall recover."* (Mark 16:17-18)

You may need to add fasting to your prayer as he said, *"However, this kind does not go out except by prayer and fasting."* (Matt 17:21) Adding fasting to prayer helps to fine tune your spirit to be able to make more power available to produce for you the results you want from your prayer.

Prayer of Salvation

In case you have been reading this book, and you are not yet born again, or you have walked away from the faith, now is the time to put things right with God. We believe this is your appointed time to receive this precious gift of eternal life and start a personal relationship with God almighty by wholeheartedly repeating the confession below:

Dear Father, thank you for loving me so much that you sent your only begotten son; that if I believe in him, I should never perish but have everlasting life.

Father as your word says if we shall confess with our mouth the Lord Jesus and shall believe in our hearts that you have raised him from the dead, we shall be saved According to Romans 10:9; I right now confess with my mouth that Jesus is my lord and savior because I believe in my heart that he died for me and you raised him from the dead for my salvation. I receive the forgiveness of all my sins today.

Thank you, dear Father, for saving my life and for the precious gift of eternal life I have received now through Jesus Christ. I declare that I am born again. I am your child with your nature and life in me.

I belong to your kingdom now. I am a new creature, the old is gone, the new has come and all the new in me now is from you, my God, in Jesus' mighty name. Amen.

Congratulations! You are now a child of God. You can reach us for more information through the contact address in this book. God richly bless you!